COMETS AND ASTEROIDS

E.M.HANS

HODDER
Wayland

An imprint of Hodder Children's Books

COMETS AND ASTEROIDS

Other titles in the series: • Constellations • The Earth •
• The Moon • The Solar System • Space Mysteries •
• Space Travel • The Sun •

© 2000 White-Thomson Publishing Ltd
This edition published in 2001.

Prepared for Hodder Wayland by
White-Thomson Publishing Ltd
2/3 St. Andrew's Place
Lewes
East Sussex
BN7 1UP

Editors: Carron Brown and Sarah Doughty
Designer: Tim Mayer
Consultants: Teresa Chilton/Julia Hey,
Jodrell Bank Science Centre

The right of E.M Hans to be identified as the author of this Work
has been asserted by her in accordance with the Copyright,
Designs and Patents Act 1988.

A Catalogue record for this book is available from
the British Library.

ISBN 0 7502 2723 0

Printed and bound in Italy by G. Canale & C. S.p.A.
Borgaro T.se (Turin)

Hodder Children's Books
A division of Hodder Headline Limited
338 Euston Road, London NW1 3BH

 CONTENTS

THE TUNGUSKA BLAST   4

COMETS; THE 'HAIRY STARS'   6

WHAT ARE COMETS?   12

THE ASTEROID BELT   16

METEOROIDS, METEORS AND
METEORITES   22

GLOSSARY   30

FURTHER INFORMATION   31

INDEX   32

THE TUNGUSKA BLAST

On 30 June 1908, something fell from the sky over Tunguska in Siberia and knocked down a whole forest. It happened just after dawn. Even 500 km away, people saw a pale blue fireball streak across the sky. It was so bright that it 'made even the Sun look dark'. The object exploded in the air with enormous force. Trees were flattened for 30–40 km from the centre of the blast. Many were torn up by the roots. All were left pointing outwards from the centre where a huge fire raged, scorching trees up to 18 km away. The explosion 'like gun-fire' was heard for thousands of kilometres. It caused a pressure wave in the atmosphere that circled the world.

The Tunguska object was probably about 50 m across and exploded 6 km above the ground.

▼ The Tunguska fireball travelled through space and exploded before reaching the ground. It was probably a small asteroid or part of a comet.

▲ The Tunguska blast destroyed thousands of square kilometres of forest.

The number of comets to hit Earth is estimated at about one every two to four thousand years.

Whatever the object was, it came from space. It must have been fairly fragile because, although it was quite large, it did not reach the ground before it exploded. There was no crater. It may have been a small asteroid or part of a comet. There are many such objects in our solar system. They orbit the Sun just as planets do and, occasionally, one of them may hit the Earth.

COMETS; THE 'HAIRY STARS'

Very few comets are harmful to the Earth. Most of them are far out in space and never come close to our planet at all.

Comet Hale-Bopp

In March and April 1997, the beautiful Comet Hale-Bopp graced our skies. It was bright enough to be seen in the night skies, even through city lights. It looked just as we expect a comet to look, with a bright star-like head surrounded by a haze and with a long trailing misty tail. It's this tail that gives rise to the name 'comet' which comes from the Greek word for hair. In the past, people thought that a comet looked like a head of long hair blowing in the wind.

A comet is generally named after the person who first sees it. Comet Hale-Bopp was discovered at the same time – but quite separately – by Mr Hale and Mr Bopp, two US amateur astronomers.

◄ Comet Hale-Bopp was one of the brightest comets of the twentieth century.

◄ This picture shows the two tails of Hale-Bopp: the blue tail is gas while the white tail is dust.

If you looked at Comet Hale-Bopp through binoculars, you would have seen two tails. One was white and slightly curved, while the other was thin, blue and straight. When the head of Hale-Bopp was examined through a telescope, something even more amazing was seen. The head looked like a bright point of light surrounded by a hazy spiral.

In 1784, a Frenchman called Jean August d'Angos 'forged' a comet. He reported seeing it and claimed it should be named after him. However no one else could find any trace of it.

Comets as bad omens

Long ago, comets were a source of great fear. They appeared unexpectedly in the sky and were thought to foretell some dreadful happening like a war or a plague. Old drawings exist showing comets in the shape of swords or other weapons. The word 'disaster' comes from the Latin for a bad star – a comet. Our word 'flu' is from an Italian idea that the 'influenza' or influence of a comet caused illness. Comets were even blamed for an outbreak of sneezing sickness among cats in Germany!

The Aztecs of ancient Mexico called comets 'smoking stars'.

▼ In Constantinople, in 1456, Halley's Comet was seen as a bad omen.

▲ This Chinese scholar is examining a celestial globe.

The Zulu people of South Africa thought that comets brought war. The Masai in East Africa said that a comet in the sky meant famine.

However, not everyone in the past worried about comets. In AD 79, the Roman emperor Vespasian said that the hairy star in the sky that year did not mean death for him. Instead, it was trouble for his enemy, the king of Parthia, since he was a hairy man and Vespasian was bald.

Chinese astronomers kept very careful records of comets long before European observers became interested. They, too, believed that comets were evil omens.

Halley's Comet

▼ Halley's Comet appeared in 1066. It is shown in the Bayeux tapestry – a warning to King Harold of England. He was overthrown by the Norman invasion of that year.

The most famous comet of all is Halley's Comet. Edmund Halley, was an Englishman, born in 1656. He did not discover the comet – but he showed that it travels around the Sun every 76 years and predicted when it would return. Up until the 1700s, people were still afraid of comets. Halley showed once and for all that they are just ordinary members of our solar system with paths around the Sun, which can be calculated like those of the planets.

▲ In 1910, Halley's Comet was photographed for the first time. It came so close to the Earth that our planet passed through its tail.

Halley said that his comet would return around Christmas, 1758. He was also able to predict where in the sky it would appear. Halley didn't live to see if his prediction came true – he died in 1742, aged 86. However, on Christmas night 1758, a German farmer who was a keen amateur astronomer found Halley's Comet just where Halley said it would be.

The last time Halley's Comet appeared in our skies was 1985–6. We will not see it again until the year 2061.

Halley's Comet has now been traced far back into the past. The oldest observations we have of it are from Babylonian clay tablets that were written in 240 BC.

The orbit of a comet is ▶ not quite the same as a planet's path around the Sun. The orbits are both elliptical but the comet's path is usually a long, thin, oval shape.

WHAT ARE COMETS?

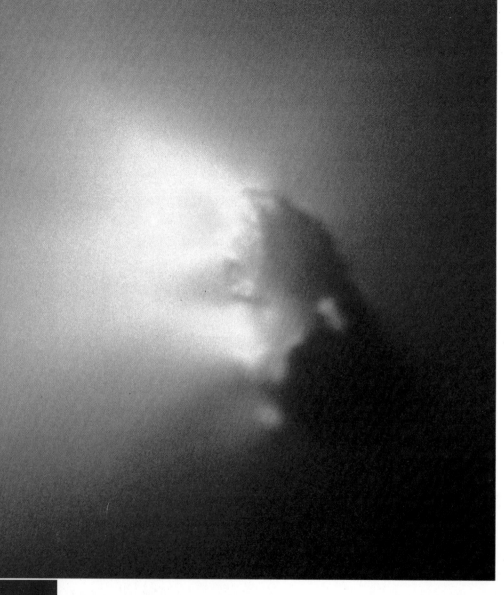

▲ In 1986, a spacecraft called *Giotto* flew into the coma of Halley's Comet to photograph its nucleus.

Comets are objects made of ice with rocks and dust embedded in them – like big dirty snowballs. They range in size from a few kilometres to a few hundred kilometres across. Despite their size, they are quite flimsy although they may contain lumps of rock. Comets have often been seen to break up. Because of their long thin orbits, comets spend most of their time far from the Sun where it is very cold. However, as a comet nears the Sun, it changes dramatically. The Sun's heat turns some of the comet's ice to gas. The comet now has a nucleus (the dirty snowball) surrounded by a cloud of gas called the coma. Dust is also released.

The spiral shape in the head of Comet Hale-Bopp was caused by a strong jet of gas given out from its spinning nucleus.

▼ Although Comet Hyakutake is only a few kilometres across, its blue gas tail is about 550 million km long.

Nearer still to the Sun, the solar wind (a stream of particles from the Sun) pushes gas and dust away from the head of the comet to form a tail. The tail always points away from the Sun. Often a comet shows more than one tail. The dust forms a yellowish slightly curved tail and the gas makes a straight thin blue tail. A comet's tail may be millions of kilometres long but its material is spread so thinly that there is almost nothing there.

Kuiper Belt and the Oort Cloud

▼ The Oort Cloud consists of billions of frozen comets. The shining star in the middle of the cloud, is the Sun.

We only see comets with their long graceful tails when they come near to the Sun. Most of them stay far out at the edge of the solar system, where they never develop tails and can only be seen with very large telescopes. We now know that there is a ring of comets, most of which are far out beyond the orbit of Pluto. This is called the Kuiper Belt. Even further out is a spherical shell of comets called the Oort Cloud.

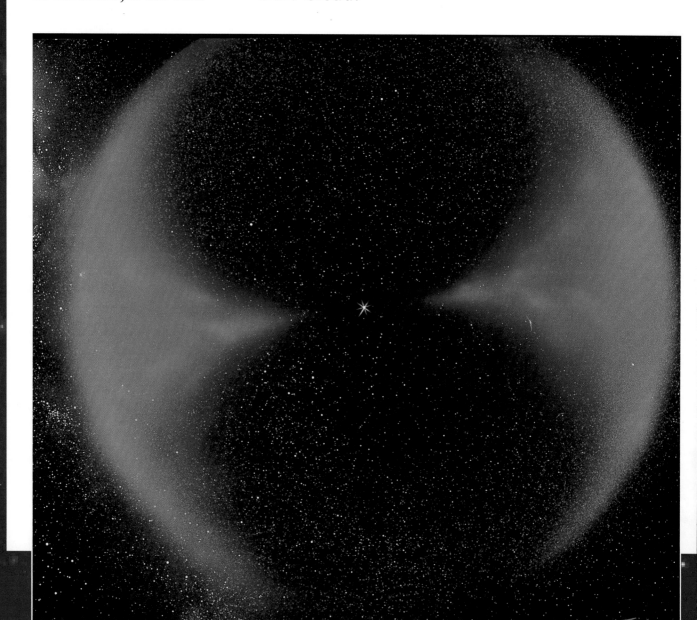

Comet Hyakutake was ▶
an unexpected visitor when
it passed within 15 million
km of Earth in 1996.

These very distant
comets may take tens
of thousands or even
millions of years to
orbit the Sun.
Occasionally, as the Sun
passes by another star
or through a cloud of gas in space, some of these
comets will be shaken from their paths. They
then plunge in towards the Sun. We do not
know when to expect these comets because
we have never seen them before and may
never see them again. If such a comet passes
close to a large planet such as Jupiter, its
orbit may be changed and it may become
trapped in the inner solar system. This is what
happened to Halley's Comet.

The Oort cloud may be
made up of debris left over
from when the
solar system was formed.

THE ASTEROID BELT

Mars

Jupiter

The asteroid belt is a ring of objects orbiting the Sun like tiny planets. Asteroids, or minor planets, are small rocky objects that range in size from a few hundred metres, up to 1,000 km across. Over 10,000 of them have been discovered so far. Most of these follow paths around the Sun between the orbits of Mars and Jupiter.

There may be up to 100 million asteroids in the main belt.

▲ Most asteroids lie between the orbits of Mars and Jupiter. A few have orbits that bring them close to Earth.

Shapes of asteroids

Only the largest asteroids are round like planets. Most of them have strange irregular shapes. All those we have photographed so far are covered in craters where other objects have hit them. Some have cracks and grooves as if they had almost been broken up. Astronomers think that our present-day asteroids were formed when much larger objects about the size of the Moon crashed into each other. Each of these larger objects had the same type of interior as the Earth – a metal core inside a rocky mantle and crust. When they were broken apart, some of the fragments were rocky, some were metallic and some were both. This explains why asteroids can have surfaces ranging from rock to iron.

▼ The asteroid belt contains thousands of rocks of different shapes and sizes resulting from past collisions.

The discovery of asteroids

Asteroids were discovered because astronomers were looking for a 'missing' planet between Mars and Jupiter. They had noticed that the distances between the planets increased as you get further from the Sun. However, the distance between Mars and Jupiter is too large to fit this pattern. Astronomers thought that there must be another planet there that nobody had yet noticed.

Asteroid hunter K. L. Hencke searched for 15 years before finding his first asteroid.

▼ Objects, such as comets or asteroids, orbit the Sun.

▼ Ceres was the first asteroid to be found. It is also the largest known asteroid with its diameter averaging 940 km.

In spite of this search, the first asteroid, Ceres, was found quite accidentally by the Italian astronomer Giuseppe Piazzi on New Year's Day, 1801. He was working on measuring the positions of stars when he noticed that one 'star' appeared to move from one night to the next. He realized that the object couldn't be a star but must be something in orbit around the Sun. After this, asteroids were found by the dozen. Soon so many had been found that is was agreed that they should be named by their discoverer. One observer, Johann Palisa, who found 125 asteroids sold the right to name one of them. He needed money for a trip to see a total solar eclipse.

▲ Vesta is the third largest asteroid and is also the brightest.

The importance of asteroids

Until recently, asteroids were not thought of as very important – they are quite small compared to planets. However, with the coming of the space age attitudes have changed. At first scientists only worried about asteroids because of the damage they might do to spacecraft. A collision with an asteroid would destroy a spacecraft; a near miss might change its orbit and send it off in the wrong direction.

The first asteroid to be photographed by a space probe was Gaspra. In 1991, Gaspra was photographed by Galileo, **on its way to Jupiter.**

▼ This is Phobos, the inner of the two moons of Mars. Astronomers call it a captured asteroid and it is 22 km across.

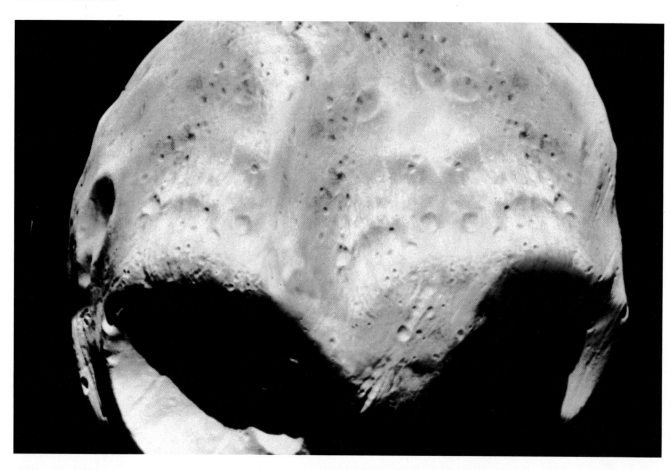

▲ The asteroid Ida has its own moon, a tiny object called Dactyl, only 1.4 km wide.

Asteroids used to be called 'the vermin of the skies' because they got in the way of studying stars and galaxies.

Today, asteroids are studied for other reasons. They can give information about the early history of our solar system and how it was formed. Perhaps in the future they can even be mined to provide metals and other minerals needed in space or on Earth.

METEOROIDS, METEORS AND METEORITES

As well as asteroids there are millions of smaller objects orbiting the Sun. These are called meteoroids. If one collides with the Earth, we see it as a meteor, the name given to the streak of light a meteoroid makes as it burns up in the Earth's atmosphere. Meteors are also called 'shooting stars' or 'falling stars' but they are not stars at all. When a meteoroid enters the Earth's atmosphere, it may be travelling as fast as 70 km per second. The friction caused by the meteoroid as it pushes through the air makes it get so hot that it burns up and produces a bright trail of light. A meteor usually lasts only a second or so before it is destroyed. Most burn up between 75 and 115 km above the ground.

Prehistoric people made weapons from iron meteorites.

◄ The best time to look for meteors is on a clear night during a forecasted meteor shower.

Meteoroids that produce meteors bright enough for us to see are usually about one centimetre across. Meteoroids smaller than this are not visible. Very large meteoroids make very bright meteors called bolides, or fireballs. These objects may be so big that they are not completely burned up before they reach the ground. The remains of meteors that hit the Earth are called meteorites. Most museums have examples of these 'stones from space'.

▼ Inside a stony-iron meteorite. This probably came from a meteoroid formed billions of years ago. It is made up of rock and metal.

On 26 April 1803, over 3,000 stones (meteorites) fell at L'Aigle in Normandy, France.

Meteor showers

On most clear nights without moonlight, we might see about ten meteors per hour. However, at certain times of the year we see many more. These events are called meteor showers. They can be very spectacular, with dozens or even hundreds of meteors every hour. The meteors of a shower all seem to come out of one point in the sky. It is just the same effect you see if you are travelling in a car during a snow storm. All the snowflakes seem to be coming at you from a point in front of the car. In reality, meteors are all entering the atmosphere from different points.

Celtic people used to believe that meteors were the souls of druids (their priests and wise men) flashing across the sky.

◀ The Leonid meteor shower occurs mid-November each year. One of the most amazing meteor storms (a very intense meteor shower) happened on 12–13 November 1833, when the Leonid meteors fell at a rate of over 15 every second.

▲ These are meteors streaking across the Earth's skies. The tails are caused by the debris burning up in the Earth's atmosphere.

The Orionid meteors in late October are produced by particles from Halley's Comet.

Meteor showers occur when the Earth, as it travels around the Sun, runs into a stream of rocks and dust left over from the break up of a comet. Meteor showers are named after the part of the sky from which they seem to come. One of the best showers to watch is the Perseid meteor shower, which happens in mid-August.

The meteors all seem to come out of the constellation Perseus. The Perseid meteors have been seen every August for thousands of years.

Huge impacts!

Most meteorites falling on the Earth are small and do no damage at all. Occasionally, though, something much bigger collides with our planet. About 50,000 years ago, an iron meteoroid 40–50 m wide struck the Earth. It produced a crater 1.2 km across and 175 m deep in what is now northern Arizona. It is called the Barringer Crater after the man who first suggested that it was made by a meteorite.

▼ When the Barringer Crater was first discovered, the area around it was covered with chunks of iron meteorites stretching for 13-16 km.

The impact of a 10-km asteroid is 100,000 times more powerful than the strongest recorded earthquakes.

▲ The impact of the asteroid that hit Earth 65 million years ago may have looked like this from space.

About 65 million years ago, a 10-km asteroid hurtled into the shallow sea that then covered the Yucatan peninsula in Mexico. It gouged out a crater 180 km wide and sent huge amounts of sea water, dust and debris up into the air. The effect was so terrible that it changed the Earth for ever. For a time the sunlight was blocked by thick clouds, so plants began to die. The rain was acidic and poisonous. Many of the animals on Earth at the time may have died out – the most famous among them being the dinosaurs. Some plants and animals survived and filled the Earth again once the clouds and rain cleared. These early animals included our own ancestors.

The largest craters on Earth (both about 300 km across) are at Uredefort in South Africa (over 2,000 million years old) and Sudbury in Canada (1,850 million years old).

The surface of the solar system

Long ago, impacts on the Earth were more common. In fact, our planet and other planets and moons of our solar system were formed by smaller objects colliding and sticking together. The Earth is mainly covered in oceans so we can only see the craters from objects which hit the land. These are all quite recent in terms of the history of our planet. However, if we look at our Moon, which has no liquid water, we can see a kind of 'fossil' which shows us how the surface of the Earth may have looked in the past. The planet Mercury is also heavily cratered. So, too, are many of the moons of the giant planets Jupiter, Saturn, Uranus and Neptune.

◀ Many of the craters on the Moon's surface were made by large meteorites hitting its surface millions of years ago.

▲ An artist's impression of part of Shoemaker-Levy-9 heading towards Jupiter. One fragment explodes and disintegrates in Jupiter's atmosphere.

Recent and future collisions

Collisions are not as frequent now but they still happen. In July 1994, the fragments of a broken comet called Shoemaker-Levy-9 smashed into the giant gas planet Jupiter. The resulting explosion produced huge dark stains on the planet that lasted for months.

In December 1994, the asteroid 1994XMI passed Earth at a distance equivalent to one-third of our own distance to the Moon.

Earth will certainly be struck again in the future. An object such as asteroid XF11, discovered in 1997 to be heading for a near-Earth encounter in 2028, would certainly do a lot of damage. Fortunately, the latest calculations show that this one will miss us!

 GLOSSARY

Asteroids Small rocks that orbit the Sun, also known as 'minor planets'.

Astronomers People who study the stars.

Atmosphere A layer of gases around a planet.

Coma A cloud of gas and dust surrounding the nucleus of a comet.

Constellation Groups of stars in the sky that make up a star picture.

Core The central part of a planet, moon or asteroid.

Crater A deep, wide hole on a surface.

Crust The outer layer of a planet, moon or asteroid.

Friction Rubbing, producing heat.

Galaxies Large groups of stars in the sky held together by gravity.

Mantle A thick layer which lies between the core and crust of a planet.

Meteor A streak of light produced by a meteoroid entering the Earth's atmosphere.

Meteorites The remains of a meteor that has fallen to Earth.

Meteoroids Solid objects drifting in space.

Moon A natural satellite that orbits a planet.

Nucleus The main, leading part of a comet, made of ice and rock.

Orbit To move around another object in space.

Particles Very small parts of an object.

Planet A body that does not give out its own light and orbits a star.

Probe An unmanned spacecraft that can find and transmit information.

Solar eclipse On Earth, this is the view of the Sun obscured by the Moon moving in front of it.

Solar system The name given to a group of planets that orbit a star.

Star A large, luminous, gaseous body in space that produces its own energy.

FURTHER INFORMATION

Web sites:

http://ispec.scibernet.com/station/asteroid.html

General information about asteroids and meteors.

http://www.jpl.nasa.gov/solarsystem/

NASA's site on the solar system, which includes comets and asteroids.

http://comets.amsmeteors.org

The comets and meteor showers site gives information on comets and meteor visits to Earth's skies.

Books to read:

Comets and Meteor Showers Paul Sipiera (Children's Press, 1997)

Comets and Shooting Stars Patrick Moore (Random House, 1998)

Comets, Meteors and Asteroids Simon Seymour (HarperCollins, 1998)

Places to visit:

Jodrell Bank Science Centre and Planetarium, Macclesfield, Cheshire (Tel: 01477 571339).

The Planetarium, Euston Road, London (Tel: 0207 935 6861).

The Royal Observatory Greenwich, London (Tel: 0208 312 6557) includes historical telescopes and has a planetarium.

The Science Museum, Exhibition Road, South Kensington, London (Tel: 0207 938 8000) includes interactive science exhibits.

COMETS AND ASTEROIDS

HISTORY
- Find historical sources (such as newspapers) relating to the Tunguska blast in 1908.
- Research meteorite impacts in history.
- Find out more about Edmund Halley (1656-1742).
- Investigate all the times in history that Halley's Comet has visited us. Make a timeline of the dates.

SCIENCE
- Watch out for meteors such as the Perseid meteor shower in August, the Orionid meteors in October, and the Leonid meteors in November.
- Investigate aspects of heating, freezing and melting. Relate this to a comet passing close to the Sun.

GEOGRAPHY
- Find photographs of the giant planets and their moons and make a list of the ones which have been the most badly hit by meteorites.
- Find out the names of the craters on the Moon.

ART AND CRAFT
- Draw your own map of the solar system with the planets circling the Sun in the correct order. Add in the asteroid belt, the Kuiper Belt, and the Oort cloud.
- Create a cratered lunar surface.

ENGLISH
- Write a fictional newspaper report about a small meteorite crashing to earth. Where did it fall and what was its impact?
- Write about the effect that a huge asteroid had on the dinosaurs and why they died out.

MATHS
- Find out about elliptical shapes and orbits.

 # INDEX

All numbers in **bold** refer to pictures as well as text.

1994-XMI 29

asteroids 4, 5, 16-21
  belt of asteroids **16, 17, 18**
  Ceres **19**
  Ida **21**
  Phobos **20**
  Shoemaker-Levy-9 **29**
  Vesta **19**

comets 4-15, 25, 29
  Hale-Bopp **6, 7,** 13
  Halley's **8, 10, 11, 12,** 15, 25
  Hyakutake **13, 15**
  nucleus of **12**
  omens 8, 9
  orbits of **11,** 12, 15
  tails of **13**

Halley, Edmund 10, 11

Jupiter 15, **16,** 17, 18, 20, 28, 29

Kuiper Belt 14

Mars 16, 18, 20
Mercury 28
meteorites **23,** 26, **28, 29**
meteoroids 22-3
meteor **22,** 23
  showers **24, 25**
minerals 21
Moon, the **28**

Oort Cloud **14,** 15

Piazzi, Giuseppe 19
Pluto 14

shooting stars 22
solar system 5, 10, 15, 21, 28
solar wind 13
Sun, the 4, 5, 10, 12, 13, **14,** 15, 16, 19, 22, 25

Tunguska blast **4, 5**

Picture acknowledgements:
The publishers would like to thank the following for allowing their pictures to be reproduced in this book: Bruce Coleman/Astrofoto 1, 14, 22, 24, cover bottom; Eye Ubiquitous cover top; Mary Evans 8, 9, 10; Genesis 20, 28; Science Photo Library/Julian Baum 29, /Chris Butler 27, /European Space Agency 12, /Jack Finch 6, /John Foster 11 bottom, /Gordon Garradd 15, /David A. Hardy 16, /Harvard College Observatory 11 top, /NASA 21, /Novosti Press Agency 5, /David Parker 26, /Pekka Parvianen 7, /Detlev van Ravenswaay 23, /Frank Zullo 3, 13; /Dr Seth Shostak 18, cover main.
Artwork by Peter Bull Art Studio.